Knowing Growing Going

How A Relationship With God
Changes Everything

ANTHONY DELANEY

Published for Anthony Delaney by Verité CM Ltd.

ISBN No: 978-1-914388-32-3

Print and production management by

Verité CM Ltd, Worthing, West Sussex BN12 4BG UK.
www.veritecm.com

About the Author

Anthony Delaney FRSA is a former police officer and serial social entrepreneur based in the UK where he leads Ivy Manchester Ltd.

His previous books include *The Man You Were Made To Be*, *Work It Out*, *Rough Diamonds* and *The BEST Marriage – Why Settle For Less?*

Why And How To Meet With Others For Knowing Growing Going

Following Jesus is a team sport! God wants to build us into a family learning to follow him together. That's why it's great to meet up with a few others or do this as a study group.

Remember that Jesus loved bringing his friends into those kind of gatherings and he has promised whenever we meet like that, even now, he'll be with us spiritually and powerfully present. Some people like to put out an empty chair to remind ourselves he's really with us.

Meet in a house, a pub, on a train, in a coffee shop, even a church if you like - and just spend a friendly hour together after each of these three sessions to put what you are learning into practice in your life.

You can so do this! Nobody needs to be any kind of expert, we are all learners, that's what the word 'disciple' actually means after all - and there's always more to learn about God.

Knowing

Welcome to this short series of thoughts about God and how you can connect with him that I've called KNOWING, GROWING, GOING.

Years ago I was at a point in life when I was young, had money, an exciting job I loved with lots of good friends. But there were times when I would be on my own and feel like there was something missing, somehow. I didn't even know what I was looking for, but there was a gap I couldn't fill with success, sex, or stuff I would buy.

I've since found out that in the Bible there was a very successful person who you could describe as the man who had it all, but he came to the same place and he writes about it in a book called Ecclesiastes where he says it just felt ultimately meaningless. Empty. When you read it you see he had incredible riches and power - but everything he grabbed for was like smoke. He knew he couldn't hold onto it.

In Chapter 1 he tried to figure it out by the pursuit of knowledge but he had to admit he wasn't clever enough to work out life, the universe and everything. That kind of knowing is only ever partial. You can have a PhD or have more degrees than a thermometer, become an expert whereby people call you a genius in some tiny portion of how things work in this great big galaxy - but the best scientists and philosophers are humble enough to not become or pretend to be a know all.

In the next Chapters he details various projects and pursuits of pleasure anyway you can imagine he went for it. But kept coming up empty again in the end. Do you know what that feels like? He played music, played around and played the fool. All empty. He worked hard as he could but then thought 'What's the point if it's all pointless – even the rich and famous end up pushing up the daisies and that could be me any day, now like everyone else.'

I'm fairly sure you've thought about the big questions too at times.

Questions like

What am I meant to do in life and what happens next?

Why am I even here?

Is God real - and if so can I know him?

The world has been through some massive shake ups in the last five years hasn't it and I don't know anyone who hasn't ended up with big questions and even concerns, together perhaps with some fears or uncertainties where we used to think everything would somehow just pan out and be all right. A recent survey called Talking Jesus where I live here in the UK said perhaps surprisingly that nearly half of the population would still describe ourselves as Christians though they're not all involved with church right now. When it came to questions about Jesus Christ 20% of people thought he was a historical figure who is actually God, and just under 30% said they believe he died and rose again like the Bible describes it.

When looking for answers to the God questions the majority of people surveyed said they would check Google and I don't know where you are at as you are at or what you'd have said to these kind of questions, but whether you have any kind of faith background right now, or you're really not sure, you are so welcome and it's great to have an open mind so thanks for checking this out with us.

So where do you start?

Well I would start with the Bible, and rather than say read the whole lot because it's a big collection of 66 books not just a book, the first place I'd say to look is the first page of the first book in what we call the Old Testament which is Genesis. The first four words are these: "In the beginning God."[1]

My dad had a wry Irish humour and if anyone was lost and pulled over to ask him for directions he might smile and say "If I were you I wouldn't start from here."

And if you want to figure out life and the galaxy and all those big questions, you need to start with something bigger than yourself. Have you heard the phrase "It does

---

[1] Genesis 1:1

not all revolve around you." That brings us down to earth with a bump because you and I are too small to make the world go round. If we just focus on ourselves we'll end up down, deluded or dizzy.

Knowing God doesn't start with us. It starts with God. And the good news we read as we carry on even a few more sentences is that this is a God who wants to be known. "In the beginning, God created the heavens and the earth." So the story of the universe is not about us. We are not the stars, God is - who it later goes on to say in quite an offhand way 'also created the stars.'[2]

Recently I spent some time walking in the mountains in Scotland and what I could from the top all around me in every direction was breath-taking. Of course it was just a fraction of creation. If I'd taken a microbe from the floor underneath me and looked in a powerful microscope I could have been stunned too at the intricacy and complexity of life all around me and all the 'it just so happens' that happened for it to happen would blow my mind so I really would not have enough faith to believe there was not a Creator for what was created around me. But at night I camped out and was even more in awe as I looked up at a sky unspoilt by light pollution realising that the millions of stars I could see were just a fraction from the galaxies in that vast canopy.

You must have had one of those 'Wow!' moments in nature?

People sometimes say "Well if God just showed himself

---

[2] Genesis 1:16

I would believe him" but I believe he does so with every dawn and dusk and every breath we take.

The technical term for that in theology is 'general revelation,' the idea that one of the things God has done so everyone can know him is leave clues all over what he made, including you and me who the Bible says he made in his image - his fingerprints are all over you. Including in your unique fingerprints and DNA.

One Bible poem starts by saying, "The heavens declare the glory of God."[3] But even if God wrote in the clouds "Hey! Here I am" few might believe it, some people would deny it, others would explain it and a lot of internet conspiracy pages would start because of it.

So the New Testament of the Bible a writer called Paul the apostle wrote that "since the creation of the world God's invisible qualities – his eternal power and divine nature – have been clearly seen, being understood from what has been made, so that people are without excuse."[4] It's like, general revelation shows me that this cosmos didn't create itself any more than I am actually a 'self made man.' But my pride doesn't want to admit that and even if I do accept that yes there might be a powerful creative 'force' somewhere aloof and alone and hopefully not too angry out there in the billions of galaxies I'm told are out there, how do I not just know that, but know him?

Well that's where Jesus comes in.

---

[3] Psalm 19:1
[4] Romans 1:20

Because Christians believe in a God so huge you could never know all about him rationally, who became small so we could know him relationally.

When we use the word 'knowing', it can apply in different ways. I know about all kinds of people because of the internet and social media probably gives us all way too much information. But I don't know them. What if knowing God is less like reading a page about him on Wikipedia and more like having a meal with someone who loves you?

Interestingly that's what Jesus Christ did a lot, 2000 years ago.

He invited people to come and hang out with him.

He even invited himself to come to their houses.

I mean the wrong kind of people as far as the religion of the day said were wrong. He got in so much trouble with them because they said he was always having too much of a good time with bad people. Though couldn't argue with the brilliance of Jesus' teaching or beat him win an argument or deny the power of his miracles, so they threw mud at him because he had this reputation of being what they called 'a friend of sinners.'

Jesus never denied that he was just that when he came to earth effectively saying 'If you want to know God, you have to get to know me.'[5]

But the way he meant knowing did not mean he would ask people to sit a theological test.

---

[5] John 14:6

He came and sat down and ate and drank with them so they would not just know about God like other religious teachers do. This kind of knowing was personal.

Nobody ever sat cross legged on top of a mountain and figured out that God would plan the whole universe in such detail and you and me with such care that he would love us enough to reach out and come to save us, even though it would cost him everything to do so.

I open my Bible and I don't just have general revelation but special revelation I could never know about God unless he showed me but it's there in black and white, that he came in flesh and blood. To live and die and rise again so I could know he is God and he good and he is real and I belong with him.

The first miracle he did was at a wedding where he made more wine so the party wouldn't stop.[6] By the way - who would make up a God like that? If you were making up stories about someone trying to prove he was God, wouldn't you come up with something like lightning striking where he pointed?

The Bible helps me see what I'd still be in the dark about even if I spent my whole life studying the stars through the most powerful telescope. That the only thing as great as his power is his love, and that's what Jesus came to show us so we could know God.

I read here that Jesus said he's the light of the world and if you follow him you'll never walk in darkness.

---

[6] John 2:1-11

I remember trying to figure out life and just getting more and more confused and worried, messed up and broken - hurting myself and others. But then I see he says things here like, 'I've come to seek out and save people who are lost, because I am the way. I am the truth that will set you free. God my Father – follow me and you call him Father too, because he loves the world so much that he sent me to save you from your sins, to be part of his family forever after."

Do you know him? Do you want to know God in relationship and reality? Tell him so now in an honest prayer from your heart in the name of Jesus, ask him to forgive what you have done wrong in the past and lead your life today and forever.

You won't be disappointed, because he will answer.

KNOWING MORE: ONE HOUR MEETING

- **READ:** John 2:1-11

- **RETELL:** the story in your own words.

  What does this tell us about Jesus?

  What does this tell me about people?

  Who do I know who needs to know these things too?

- **PRACTICE:** Draw the 3 Circles like you saw in the video and explain it to a partner.

- **PRAY:** Here's a great prayer straight from the Bible. Ask aloud that God the Father, in the name of Jesus will fill you with his Holy Spirit so you will KNOW him better.
  (See Ephesians 1:17)

  Wait a while, he will answer!

- **HOMEWORK:** This week in your own time read from John's gospel, one chapter a day, chapters 1 to 7. Ask God to speak to you and help you know him better every day.

Growing

How do we GROW the relationship God has with us when we have come to KNOW him?

Well we have seen that the kind of knowing God wants is not built on what we know in our heads, but what is happening in our hearts. The Bible simply tells us that love is the evidence that we know God, because "God is love."[7] It doesn't say 'love is god.' Love is defined by God not just because of what he does, but because of who he is - love is God's very nature. That means knowing God is not so much about what I say or think I know, it's all about love.

Writing to some early believers the apostle Paul said that knowledge, even knowledge about God, can inflate us with our own importance and pride, but love builds us and others up.[8] We grow in the love of God, by showing it, by loving others not only in words and talk but in truth and action.[9]

---

[7] 1 John 4:8

[8] 1 Corinthians 8:1

[9] 1 John 3:18

We have become accustomed to the idea that love is just a feeling I might have sometimes in some ways for some people. But when God speaks about love in the Bible he doesn't just suggest it, he commands it. In fact the greatest commandment, reiterated in various ways and times in the Bible, is to love.

One day when Jesus was being grilled by various religious theology 'experts', one asked him, out of all the things God commanded - what was most important? His reply is very simple to understand but not always easy to do, "You must love the Lord your God with all your heart, all your soul, all your mind, and all your strength." Then he added, "The second is equally important: Love your neighbour as yourself. No other commandment is greater than these"[10]

Notice that love hear effects the whole of a person. Your heart, soul and strength not just your mind. Unfortunately it seems all too often the church has made knowing God all about what we think and it's become possible even for church going people to sing many words about God, listen to too many sermons about love, but not go on and obey them by loving others. Preaching means nothing until we practice.

Jesus made this very clear through this story,

"Why do you call me, "Lord, Lord," and do not do what I say? As for everyone who comes to me and hears my words and puts them into practice, I will show you what they are like. They are like a man building a house, who

---

[10] Mark 12: 30-31

dug down deep and laid the foundation on rock. When the flood came, the torrent struck that house but could not shake it, because it was well built. But the one who hears my words and does not put them into practice is like a man who built a house on the ground without a foundation. The moment the torrent struck that house, it collapsed and its destruction was complete.'[11]

The places where Christianity is flourishing and spreading rapidly around the world are not those places where people sit around all day having theological discussions about what a passage like this means and picking apart the original language it was written in. It's where they do what Jesus said. In the West we have tried to build church on the shifting of a knowledge based system, where people hear and hear but do nothing about it, instead of an obedience based approach. But God doesn't just want us to hear what he says, he wants us to do it.[12]

Sermons galore have been preached on that story saying things like, "If you try to build your life on sex or money, power or fame - it's sinking sand." While that's completely true, it's not what Jesus was saying that day. The only difference according to Jesus between the wise man and the foolish man in this story was that the wiseman heard the words of Jesus and immediately put them into practise! He did not just hear and do nothing about it, he obeyed because he did something. That is the difference that makes all the difference.

---

[11] Luke 6:46-49

[12] James 1:22

I am not growing in God unless I am growing in love. Anything I think or say that I know about God that does not cause me to love him more or others better, is useless. Growing spiritually means closing the gap between what I say I know and how I live and love.

So if God commands me to love him and others, and love is not primarily about how I feel but what I do – how do I grow? Well a key word Jesus used there is 'practice.' I remember when I was first learning to drive and everything felt very alien, clunky and, well - mechanical. But with practice, I now do those same things automatically and subconsciously.

God gives us various practices that if we do them regularly enough will begin to change us in ways that we might now think we could never change and we will look at some of them and learning to drive is a great picture of what that relationship looks like followers of Jesus are called his 'disciples' and that word means we are constant learners.

So there are practices like regular prayer and reading the Bible for ourselves and connecting in community with others that really help us grow but before getting into that, we need to realise that rather than just give us a list of things to do or not do, God gives us the actual power we need to be able to do them.

The car and therefore the driver is useless unless it has what it needs, the power to get moving. So when we are ready for that new life and God doesn't just give us a set of instructions – that's religion. He comes to live inside us, in the person of his Holy Spirit – that's relationship.

Haven't there been things in your life you wish you could change but no matter how hard you tried you end up back at square one? Me too!

Knowing God starts with realising he is my Father and he loves me but I have been going in the wrong direction, away from him rather than to him. I'm stuck. I need to turn around, asking him to forgive my desire to make life all about me, and the wrong actions that inevitably result. The Father's answer to that prayer is that he sent Jesus Christ who shed his blood on a cross so my past could be wiped away and I can have a fresh start. I say I want to put him in the driving seat of my life, so he rules over me now and I can love God and others with all my heart, soul and mind and strength. But I know I can't do it!

I ask for help to live that new life, and the answer to that prayer is the Holy Spirit. God comes to live inside of us in a way that I have seen children just accept easily by faith – perhaps that's why Jesus loved their teachability - while adults sometimes try and fail to rationalise but the evidence it happened is seen when you have new desires that replace the old ones, new power where you used to feel weak and helpless, new love where there used to be bitterness.

Because at times you may have tried to change things on the outside but it didn't work and you couldn't, but now you have God changing you from the inside out as he makes you a new creation, still you – but more and more like Jesus every day until the day you meet him face to face.

The first disciples didn't actually call themselves Christians, that was what other people called them. The word actually means 'little Christ" and it happened when outsiders saw that all these different people whether they had been rich or poor, male or female, slaves or free, regardless of sexual history or social status, those who loved Jesus grew more and more like him. He had said that's what happens to disciples, they become like their teacher.[13]

So they forgave like he did, whether or not people deserved it. They were holy, which doesn't mean they were the kind of people you didn't want to be around because you felt bad but rather the kind of people when you were around them you felt God. They had a peaceful confidence that no matter what happened they trusted God even when they were betrayed or persecuted like he had been. They prayed and saw miracles happen, they loved and received those whom everyone else rejected. They were generous and shared joyfully with everyone who had need. Just like Jesus. That's what 'Growing' means for disciples. Being just like Jesus.

Now I know even when I say that, how very far short I myself fall short of the perfection Jesus embodied in his sinless life and glorious example – even though for over 30 years now I would say I have been a 'Christian.' The little Christ in me needs to grow an awful lot bigger so more people see the difference. But while I know I'm not what I want to be, I'm certainly not who I used to be

---

[13] Luke 6:40

either – though I suppose the best people to ask whether or not that's true would be those who know me best.

When the Bible wants to describe how this Growing happens, the image that's most often used is of some kind of fruit. Jesus said he's the vine and we are the branches.[14] We can't do anything by ourselves but when we connect and stay connected to him, his life flows through us so over time much fruit grows.

The fruit God wants to grow in our lives is also described at 'the fruit of the Spirit.' Imagine how your life and mine would be different, how the whole world would be changed if we his disciples grew so others noticed and saw that we belong to Jesus because we are continually growing in *'love, joy, peace, patience, kindness, goodness, faithfulness, gentleness and self control.'*[15]

If you want some of that growing in you – why don't you pray now and ask God's Holy Spirit to come and change you from the inside out?

A simple prayer I have prayed many times just goes like this to start you off:

'Lord come and do in me anything you need to do, so that you can do through me everything you want to do. Amen!'

---

[14] John 15:1-5

[15] Galatians 5:22-23

GROWING DEEPER: ONE HOUR MEETING

- **RECAP:** How did you get on last week? Did you get chance to share what you are learning about Jesus with anyone?

- **READ: John 15:1-17**
  What does this tell us about God?
  What does this tell me about myself?
  What does this tell me about growing?
  Who do I know who needs to know these things?

- **PRACTICE:** Write out and discuss some ways you can show love practically this week to those around you. Next week ask how it went!

- **PRAY:** for one another to be filled with the Holy Spirit of God, so that his fruit as described in Galatians 5 grows supernaturally, and shows super fast!

- **HOMEWORK:** Keep reading a chapter a day of John's gospel, asking God to speak to you through it so you GROW.
  Go to God in prayer daily (Philippians 4:6).
  Read the Bible daily (Acts 17:11).
  Obey God moment by moment (John 14:21).
  Witness for Christ with your life and words (John 15:8).

Going

BC

I was raised in a good family and when I was a little boy I used to just naturally say my prayers at bedtime. I had this instinctive sense that God was real so I'd talk with him and the school I went to told us stories about Jesus who I thought was pretty cool, but not as cool as Spiderman or the Hulk. As I went into my teens I began to see that the people I knew put all of those characters in the make believe category and just got on with life, I did too.

When I became a police officer I saws that there were bad guys out there, and naturally thought of myself as one of the good guys, comparing myself to the criminals I arrested. It was a tough job and I also partied hard, and I was not proud of some of the things I did both on and off duty, though on the outside everything was fine. On the inside I was cynical, nasty and a ticking time bomb of anger.

JC

One night in a nightclub I met a girl who when I later tried to ask on a date seemed very different, when I asked why she said she was a Christian and was trying to figure out what that meant. I told her that of course I was a deeply spiritual person and a Christian myself, so why didn't we learn together – starting with going to the pub? She refused graciously but said there was something happening at a church near her house, why not come along? I agreed on the basis this was one step closer to a date in my mind.

I went along and heard good music, a friendly welcome, and a compelling message. The speaker talked about how Jesus Christ is not just an historical figure, a moral teacher, a misunderstood miracle worker, or a good man. He talked about the God-man, completely human and fully God at the same time, who claimed to give life that lasts forever to people,[16] to be able to forgive sins,[17] to be the King who would one day judge of all people.[18] He said Jesus was the way to God, not just teach a way, but declaring "I am the way, the truth, the life"[19] so that whoever believed in him would live forever.[20]

The speaker said these claims are the reason he was wrongly arrested, tried and executed in the most painful and tortuous way humanity ever invented. That we get the word excruciating from the crucifixion, death on a cross where even as he was nailed Jesus forgave those

---

[16] John 10:30

[17] Mark 2:7

[18] Matthew 25:31-46

[19] John 14:6

[20] John 14:1-3

who were doing it. But he said this was no sad tale of injustice, of what can happen to the innocent when evil so often triumphs in this world. Jesus predicted it all and it fulfilled in great detail prophecies written down even centuries before he was born, that he would die in that way to give his life as a ransom to set us free, and then prove it all when he rose from the dead that Easter Day.

I didn't believe it as he said it but when he talked about the courage and love of Jesus something started to soften in my cold hard heart. Over the next few weeks I decided to read the Bible. One verse stood out and became what I call my life verse, 'Then he called the crowd to him along with his disciples and said: "Whoever wants to be my disciple must deny themselves and take up their cross and follow me."'[21] A few days after reading that, driving in my car on the way to work at the police station, listening to some music like I had heard that night that someone had put on a tape for me, I began to become more aware of the presence of God right there with me.

I pulled over, and became terribly aware of the mess I was making of my life but as I closed my eyes I somehow saw the cross, and knew that it didn't just happen to show how much he loved me, but also how desperately I needed God to save me. Even when I was a little boy I had heard that 'Jesus died for the sins of the world' but right there and then for the first time it was personal, it meant me. Things I had thought and said and done (that I had excused as I'd pointed to those others I thought must be worse) were now so clearly wrong I knew if God

---

[21] Mark 8:34

condemned me forever for them he would be completely justified. But just as I was about to give way to despair, waves of mercy and grace washed over me and I felt clean on the inside and out. It took my breath away. I knew he died for my sins, and now he was alive again, and right there with me.

A small voice sounded inside me reassuring me that I was loved, forgiven, free, accepted, and God wasn't at all done with me – in fact he had a plan for my life that was just getting started!

AD

Jesus has transformed my life in every way since then and I never want him to stop doing so! In case you're wondering, I married the girl from the club, stayed in the Police and lived out and shared my faith in the years after that with many people in need, as well as colleagues and criminals.

A decade later I began full time church ministry and that adventure of following the call of God has led me to adventures on various continents speaking to huge crowds or small meetings, seeing him at work in miraculous ways and knowing his love and faithfulness through tears and trials, joys and answered prayers. Following Jesus is not always easy of course but I have peace where I used to have pain, access to his wisdom where I used to have confusion, his strength for my weaknesses, his love for those who have hurt me, and his amazing grace for all the times I let him down and I have no fear of death because my best friend has prepared a place for me with him where I will be forever.

That's why I do this. That's why I wanted to tell you my story of what my life was like **BC** – Before Christ, how I met **JC** – Jesus Christ, and the way he changed and is still changing me as I live a new life, **AD**.

You know don't you that every time you write or see a date on a calendar you confirm the existence of JC - Jesus Christ? All of our history is divided between BC and AD – before Christ lived and after. Everyone who has met him and knows him now in real relationship will have a story to tell about how they came to know him and the difference it made. It may not be some dramatic tale about how you once were doomed in a Turkish prison when a light burst in. But if you know Jesus and have made him the star, it's a great story because of the leading man. If you have not yet done that you can meet him right now and ask him to lead your life and it's the best thing you'll ever do. The only regret I have is that I didn't somehow do it sooner because all the greatest screw ups of my life have come from when I was in charge of it.

In telling you my story even though I was a police officer I haven't been trying to convince you as if I am some expert or prosecuting or proving my case. Jesus didn't ask us to do that, he is God and he is perfectly capable of showing up in anyone's life and proving it. I don't have to be a lawyer, but he said when the Holy Spirit comes to live in us then we will receive power to be his *witnesses* near and far, wherever we are.[22]

---

[22] Acts 1:8

I can tell you what witnesses do. They tell the truth when called upon about what they have personally seen, heard and experienced. That's what I just tried to do when I told you my Jesus story and you can do the same if you met him and he's started to change your life.

You don't have to be a theological academic, you don't have to have led a terrible life or a good life 'BC.' But you have a story to tell about that. And now somehow you have come to hear the good news about Jesus and it's too good to keep to yourself.

Your family and friends and people at work and even strangers you meet are often far more ready than we realise for some good news, especially in this world right now where we seem to lurch from disaster to tragedy to chaos and back again. But you know a God who is large and in charge no matter what and you can practice telling the story of why no matter what you have confidence and faith inside you no matter what happens around you.

God says we should be ready to share the hope he has put inside of us.[23] That assumes that we are living as people of hope and you can when you're a person with faith!

So how can you be ready? Practice! I have told what I now call my "BC-JC-AD" story with many thousands of people young and old in all kinds of ways and places and it never gets old to me. When I first started to follow Jesus I had people challenge me, asking if I'd gone

[23] 1 Peter 3:15

crazy or joined a cult. I found the best answer was to tell them my story in a non-defensive way, I'd just say "Well can I tell you what happened?" That led to many more questions and often interest from the other person, because they could see Jesus was changing me life even if they wouldn't admit it yet!

Just before Jesus left to go to heaven, he gathered his friends together to tell them what to do until he comes back. There were only a handful, none of them had followed him perfectly, they had all chickened out when he was arrested and crucified but when he rose again he came and sought them out and gathered them together just like he promised.

This is described as a literal mountain top experience, and they worshipped him there. But he didn't want them to stay on that mountain with them, though I'm sure that's all they wanted. They loved KNOWING him. They wanted to just stay there as a little group of his friends GROWING their spiritual life. But he knew that real growing only comes when we get GOING.

He told those disciples to get going - to go down off the mountain they were on and take him to people of every nation all across the world. He said to his disciples "Go - and make disciples" and promised that when they did that, then they would find he really would be with them, as he is with us too, always.

GOING FURTHER: ONE HOUR MEETING

- **RECAP:**

  How did you get on last week in showing love in a practical way? Share what happened.

- **READ:** John 9:1-25

  Retell the story in your own words.

  What does this tell us about God?

  What does this tell us we should do to love God and people better?

  Who do you know who needs to hear about this?

- **THINK:** about your own BC-JC-AD story. Write it out if you can, keep it short and simple, what was life like before you met with Jesus? How did it happen? What difference is it making now?

- **PRACTICE:** Share your story out loud in response to the other person asking "So what do you mean, you're a Jesus follower now?"

- **PRAY:** For one another, for the Holy Spirit to fill you with boldness and courage as you share your story in the weeks ahead with others who are ready for some good news.